tell me abou
KRISH

ANURAG MEHTA

Nita Mehta™ WISKIDZ
ENRICHING YOUNG MINDS

An Imprint of Nita Mehta Publications

tell me about
KRISHNA

Nita Mehta Publications
Enriching Young Minds

Nita Mehta Books
Distributors & Publishers

Nita Mehta Publications
3A/3, Asaf Ali Road, New Delhi 110 002

Revised Edition 2017
Printed in India at Pushpak Press Pvt. Ltd., New Delhi.

Editorial and Marketing office
E-159, Greater Kailash II, New Delhi 110 048

Typesetting by National Information Technology Academy
3A/3, Asaf Ali Road, New Delhi 110 002

Distributed by :
NITA MEHTA BOOKS
3A/3, Asaf Ali Road, New Delhi - 02

Distribution Centre :
D16/1, Okhla Industrial Area, Phase-I,
New Delhi - 110020
Tel.: 26813199, 26813200
E-mail: nitamehta.mehta@gmail.com
Website: www.nitamehta.com

Contributing Writers:
Subhash Mehta
Tanya Mehta

Editorial & Proofreading:
Rajesh
Ramesh

Price: Rs. 395/-   US $ 15.95   UK £ 12.95

Contents

Introduction

Krishna, the dark one, being an incarnation of Lord Vishnu, is divine on one hand and endearingly human on the other. He is at once the beloved child, the stealer of hearts, the loyal friend, the simple cowherd, the great philosopher and the valiant hero. Krishna slips into each of these roles with great ease. He, however, does not perform any gimmicks or miracles (except when he wants to reveal his true form to his devotees). Krishna's miracles emerge out of a process, where he waits for the right time to come forward and fix things. Thus, his growing up is an ordinary as anyone else, rendering the message that no one can escape time or destiny.

Kansa, the Cruel King

Thousands of years ago the subjects of the kingdom of Mathura were very unhappy.

"Our King, the evil Kansa, is so cruel," said one hapless citizen.

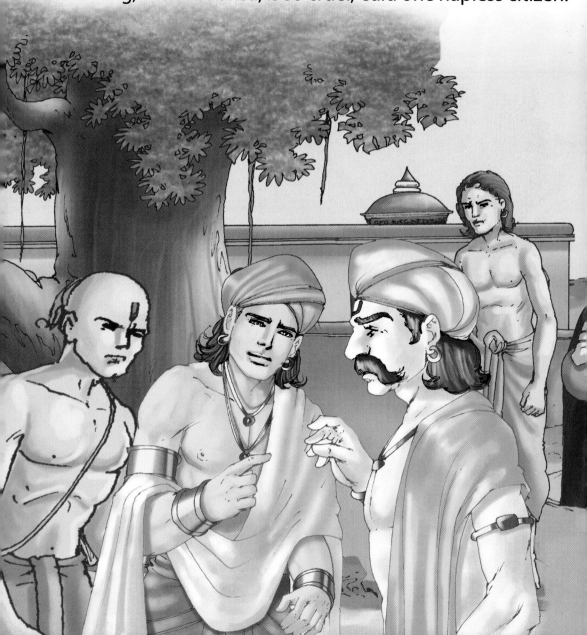

"Oh, he usurped his own father, the good king, Ugrasena and imprisoned him to capture the throne. No one can expect kindness from such a malicious king," grieved another citizen. "When Kansa was born, it was predicted that he would be a wicked soul.

Just because his parents loved him so much, they over looked his malevolent nature," whispered one of the citizens. The common people of Mathura felt helplessly subjugated by Kansa. "Who will save us from this terrible ruler?" they wailed constantly.

Vishnu

High above in the heavens, cosmic powers were gathering enough evidence against Kansa.

"Seeing Kansa increasing his evil deeds so rapidly, it will soon be time for me to descend on earth," said Lord Vishnu to his wife Goddess Lakshmi. Who is Lord Vishnu? He is one of the main Gods of the Hindu religion. Also known as the God of Preservation, he preserves whatever is created in the Universe, by Lord Brahma, the creator.

Lord Vishnu decided to come to earth as Krishna. Owing to the rules of the cosmic orders, he just could not descend as an adult. He needed to go through the whole process of taking birth on earth as a part of creation, then grow up to preserve what he was setting out to do. For this, Lord Vishnu had to plan where he wanted to be born. "I have to stay close to Kansa. I will be born in his household as a son, to Devaki, his sister. Devaki's destiny begins now. The first step is for her to be married," Vishnu concluded after much consideration.

"I will take birth from her womb, when the time is right," decided Vishnu.

Devaki & Vasudeva

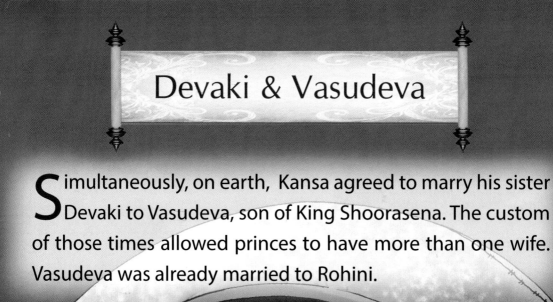

Simultaneously, on earth, Kansa agreed to marry his sister Devaki to Vasudeva, son of King Shoorasena. The custom of those times allowed princes to have more than one wife. Vasudeva was already married to Rohini.

Rohini stayed at Gokula, a small town near Mathura. Rohini's brother was Nanda, the headman of Gokula. "Spare no expense at this wedding, it has my blessings!"

Kansa pompously told his attendants. True to his orders, the wedding was a grand affair. Later, Kansa drove the newlyweds home in his carriage.

Suddenly, thunder clapped and the horses reared, neighing in a terrible shriek. Even as Kansa controlled the horses, a voice hauntingly warned from the darkening skies,

"You are doomed, Kansa. Here begins the curse! Vasudeva and Devaki's son will bring about your death!" Kansa reacted defensively, "No! Never! I will kill Devaki! If Devaki dies, the curse will break!"

Roughly pushing Devaki off the chariot, Kansa raised his sword to behead her.

"Please, please don't kill my wife,"

Vasudeva screamed clinging to Kansa's feet.

Kansa's ego swelled, hearing Vasudeva beg. He arrogantly voiced, "Go! I will not kill your wife, but for sparing her life, I will take the life of every child born to her!"

Saying that, Kansa commanded his guards to arrest Devaki and Vasudeva. The couple were chained and thrown into the prison dungeons.

Devaki & Vasudeva's Seven Children

Soon, Devaki was pregnant. Kansa was closely following the arrival of her baby.

When Devaki finally gave birth to a baby, a guard ran to inform Kansa. Kansa raced down the dungeon corridors. He grabbed the new born baby and dashed it against the wall; killing the baby instantly.

After witnessing this horrible incident, Devaki and Vasudeva prayed intensely, begging for some respite from this appalling situation. Consequently, the cruel Kansa, killed all six children born to them. When Devaki was pregnant for the seventh time, a peculiar event happened. Strangely, when it was time for the child to take birth, *no baby emerged!*

Enraged, Kansa demanded to know where the baby had disappeared from Devaki's womb. Devaki and Vasudeva had no answers. However, legend says that the baby was transferred to Vasudeva's first wife, Rohini's womb, due to the couple's intense prayers. The child born would be called Balaram.

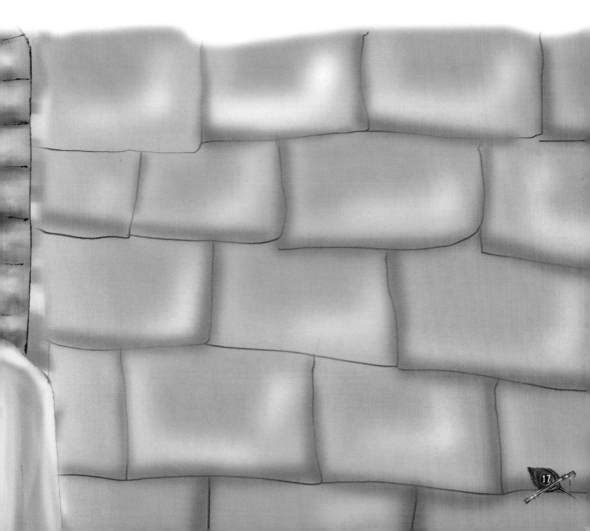

Vishnu Meets Shiva

At last, Vishnu announced, "The time has come for me to leave the heavens now and put an end to Kansa's cruelties." Before leaving, Vishnu decided to meet Shiva. Shiva is a part of the main Hindu Gods' Trinity. Reaching the snow capped mountains where Shiva lives, Vishnu greeted him.

"Welcome Vishnu! What brings you here?" asked Shiva. "I have come to inform you that I am going to earth to take another *avataar*." *Avataar* means reincarnation. Whenever there is chaos and evil prevalent on earth, Lord Vishnu takes an *avataar* to protect earthlings. "Really?" Shiva queried.

"Yes! King Kansa has become a tormentor for the people. It is time to intervene now," answered Vishnu. "Good. So who are you going as now?"

"As Krishna. I will be born to Devaki and Vasudeva…," Vishnu, in detail, informed Shiva of his plans.

After hearing him out, Shiva smiled, "Expect a visit from me Vishnu, I want to see you as a baby!"

"Yes, dear Shiva, you are most welcome. But remember, I will be baby Krishna on earth. One more thing, though I will be born to Devaki and Vasudeva at Mathura, I shall be brought up at Gokul by my foster mother, Yashodha. So, come to Gokul to meet me."

Shiva nodded as Vishnu bid a farewell and left.

The Eighth Born

It was a dark, rainy night, when the eighth child was born. Baby Krishna's advent on earth unfolded showers of flowers, brilliant light and a halo gracing his head. Devaki and Vasudeva instantly realized that this was no ordinary baby. Then to their amazement, the baby metamorphosed into the radiant form of Lord Vishnu and his resplendent presence filled the dingy dungeon cell.

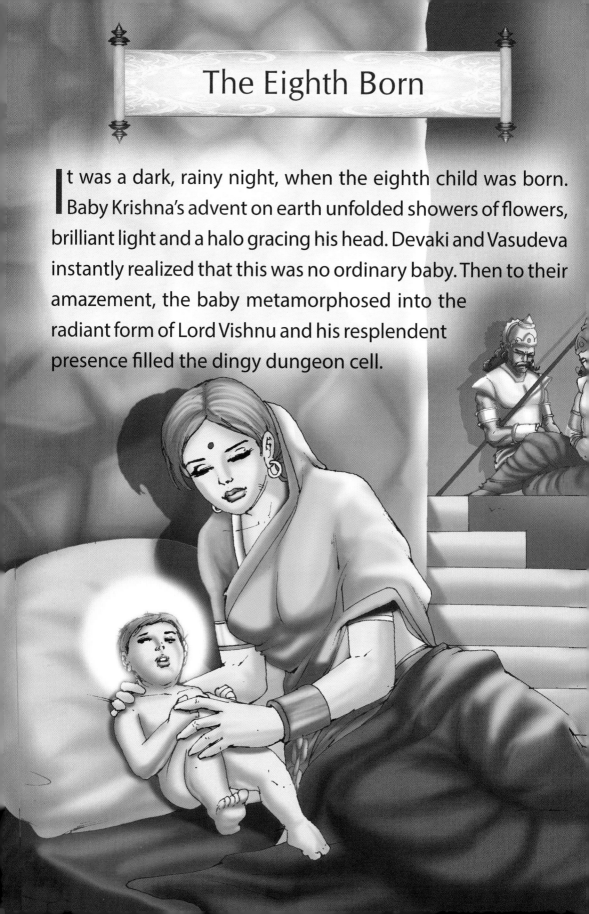

Devaki and Vasudeva gaped in awe as Vishnu in a melodious voice instructed, "Take the child to Gokul, to Nanda's house. This child is Krishna, my *avataar* (reincarnation)." Just as soon, as the vision of Vishnu dissolved, Vasudeva noticed that his chains had been magically released. Freed of shackles, Vasudeva ran to the grills of the cell. *The cells locks were all open!*

Vasudeva uttered, "We have to get this baby out of here. I will take him to Gokul immediately."

Devaki quickly found a small basket at the corner of the cell and placed the baby into the basket. Vasudeva positioned the basket on his head and walked out. The first thing he noticed was that all *the prison guards were asleep!* Vasudeva's feet automatically stepped towards river Yamuna's swirling currents. A storm was whipping up. He walked his way through rain and wind. The blinding storm, however, was making it impossible for Vasudeva to proceed. Abruptly, a thousand headed mystical serpent rose in a luminous sparkle, from out of the darkness. This was *Ananta,* Lord Vishnu's serpent. The cobra spread its hood like an umbrella protecting Vasudeva and the baby from the torrential rains. "The snake is protecting Krishna from the rains!" Vasudeva thought with wonder. Vasudeva was amazed with these strange happenings. "There is so much of light…," Vasudeva uttered when he gazed up at the sky. Through the night darkness, the moon and the millions of stars brightened their light, to guide Vasudeva's steps to Gokul.

When Vasudeva reached the Yamuna river's shore, he halted, wondering how he would resume his journey through the river without a boat. Just then, the stormy, gushing waters of the Yamuna parted and made a pathway for him to go through. Unhesitating, Vasudeva continued his journey through this path. Once he reached ashore, Vasudeva quickly left the snake and moved down the lanes of Gokul and found Nanda's house. Nanda was Vasudeva's first wife, Rohini's, brother. Vasudeva stealthily entered and switched Krishna with Nanda's new born daughter.

Nanda and Yashoda were sleeping that time and without anyone knowing, Vasudeva took their baby and sped back to the palace. The next morning, when Yashoda held her baby, she exclaimed to her husband, "That is strange! Last night when our baby was born, I could have sworn it was a girl! How come we have a son now?"

Nanda too was perplexed. However, being simple folks they accepted what they thought was their own mistake and drew the cherubic boy lovingly into their arms, unquestioningly.

Meanwhile, Vasudeva had returned to the palace safely. His chains and shackles were back in place, when the guards woke up. The cries of the baby girl alerted them. Within seconds, Kansa barged into the room.

"Give me that baby," Kansa roughly snatched the child from Devaki's lap. "Brother, it is a girl, not a boy. Please, let her live," Devaki begged. Kansa snarled, "I am taking no chances. Give her to me!" Seizing the baby, Kansa swirled the baby and dashed her against the wall. She did not die. Instead, she transformed into a eight armed Goddess, Goddess Shakti (the shakti or energy of Lord Vishnu).

"You fool! Devaki's eighth born was a son! He is safe at Nanda's house in Gokul! Watch out for your destruction," the Goddess howled in warning. Saying this, the Goddess vanished, leaving a scared and frustrated Kansa behind.

At Gokul

"We shall name him Krishna, meaning 'the dark skinned one,'" Yashoda chuckled to her husband, as this name sprang into her mind. Their lives were full and busy ever since Krishna had arrived. Baby Krishna's chortling and gurgling sounds filled the entire hut. Gokul was a small hamlet, near Mathura, where the main occupation was farming and cattle rearing. The cattle provided milk, as well as helped in furrowing the fields. Hence, inhabitants of Gokul spent most of their time at this job. Yashoda assisted her husband Nanda too. Now with a baby to care for, Yashoda found herself frantically trying to balance her tasks. Rohini, Vasudeva's first wife, often walked across to Yashoda's house with her son Balaram. Yashoda and she would exchange notes about their babies and assist each other in chores.

The Demoness

Back in Dwarka, Kansa was trapped in the throes of anxiety. He could not get the voice of Goddess Shakti out of his head. "She said Devaki's son is alive. He is in Gokul! He is the one who will kill me. Did I really hear her? Or was I imagining things?" muttered Kansa circling the palace halls, causing utter consternation amongst his courtiers. At last, he ordered his spies to find out about any strange happenings at Gokul.

They were promptly back, reporting a strange transformation at Nanda's house. "His wife gave birth to a girl. But the next day, the girl transformed into a boy!" Putting two and two together, Kansa figured out that his slayer had indeed taken birth. Kansa's edgy mind churned out an evil plot to get rid of his nemesis.

"Call Putana, the demoness," Kansa bellowed. Putana, a fiendish demoness, came quickly at his summons. "Disguise yourself and go to Gokul.

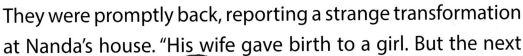

Find Nanda's house and kill their child called Krishna. You would be handsomely rewarded for this task," Kansa ordered. Putana went to Gokul to carry out her task. On reaching the gates of Gokul, she transformed herself into a beautiful local woman and asked the whereabouts of Nanda's house from the villagers. Eventually, she made her way there. Knocking at Nanda's door, she greeted Yashoda, who was holding Krishna. "I need work…," Putana sadly said, with tears in her eyes. "Oh dear, why are you crying?" Yashoda asked in concern. "Sorry, I just lost my baby and seeing you holding this child only brings back memories." Simple Yashoda's heart melted and she handed Krishna to her, saying, "Hold him as much as you want!"

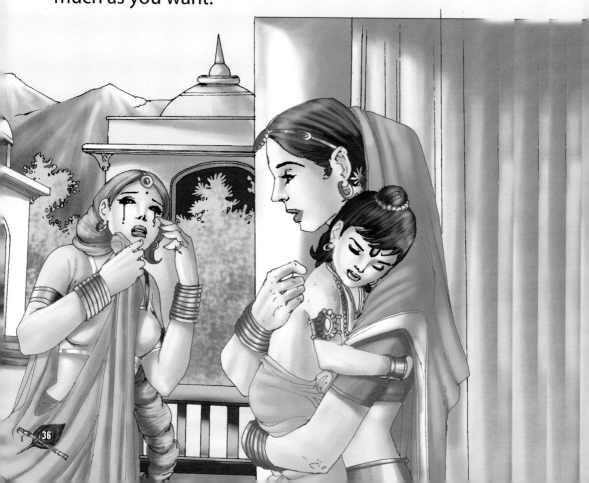

Seeing that the woman was so happy with Krishna, Yashoda trustingly decided to step out for a while to run some errand; leaving the baby in her care.

Of course, she did not catch the evil gleam in Putana's eyes when she turned to leave. As soon as Yashoda left, Putana lifted Krishna and ran out of the house. Finding an isolated knoll, she sat cross legged and began to breast-feed Krishna.

She had poisoned her own milk by magic! Her plan was to poison Krishna to death. At first, she waited for Krishna to have his fill. Krishna happily burbled, waving his legs as he drank. He drank and drank and drank! Putana started to feel dizzy, but Krishna did not stop.

Putana struggled and tried to push him away but could not. Soon, Krishna drank the life out of her and Putana fell on the ground. As soon as Putana died, she turned into her true form of a demoness. Meanwhile, Yashoda and Nanda discovered that Krishna was missing.

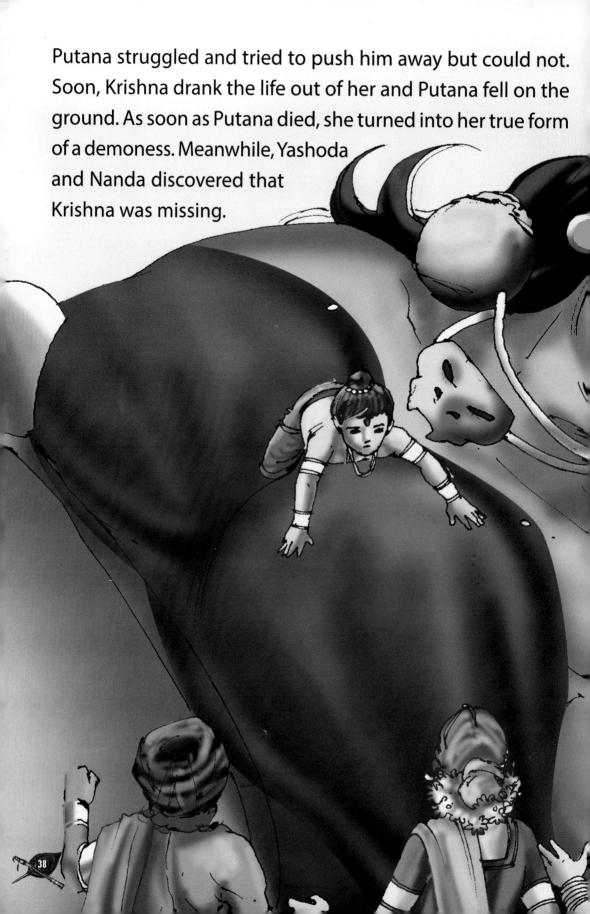

Their panic stricken cries initiated a search party. The party along with Krishna's parents finally reached the knoll. Krishna lay peacefully smiling and playing with his toes. Besides him lay the lifeless form of Putana. Yashoda gathered Krishna in her arms and vowed never to leave him alone again!

Krishna Kills Satasura

An undeterred Kansa did not cease his attempts and plots to get rid of Krishna. Soon, his next plot to kill Krishna unfolded. Since Yashoda worked in the fields along with all the other mothers, they had devised a way to keep their children with them as they laboured. Some tied a hammock to make mock cribs, while others slung their babies on their backs.

One day, Yashoda arriving at the field, saw a cart parked by a tree. "I will make Krishna rest here," she whispered as she transferred a sleeping Krishna from her arms and placed him under the shade provided by the cart. Satasura, another mate of Kansa was just waiting for this. He was an evil demon sent to Gokul to kill Krishna. Turning himself into a huge bird, Satasura perched himself on the cart. He began to rock the cart so it would topple over Krishna and kill him!

The rocking of the cart accelerated and woke Krishna up. Baby Krishna with one tiny leg, kicked the cart so hard that Satasura lost his balance and fell on the ground. That very moment, the cart also crashed atop him, killing him instantly. Hearing the crashing sounds, Yashoda, apprehensively, rushed to Krishna. Folding him in her arms, she checked and rechecked his limbs, thanking the Lord that he was unhurt!

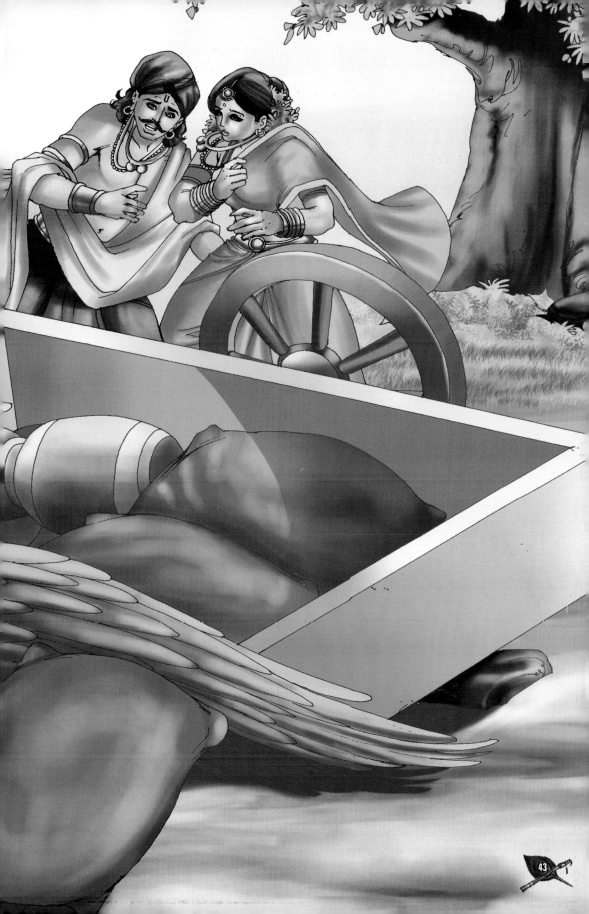

Another Attempt

"My little angel…oh, I love you so!" Yashoda sang to Krishna as she sat on the doorstep of her hut.

"TTTTTRRRRRRGH-BURMMMMMMMM!" a dark smothering dust storm whirled in a menacing dance into the courtyard.

Before Yashoda could react, the mass of wind clumped into a twirling body of clouds and seized Krishna from her lap.

"Help! My baby...the wind has taken my baby!" shrieked Yashoda. But her baby could be seen no where. The mass of clouds, in a hollow rumble, had swirled and disappeared leaving behind raging winds. Running and collecting everyone, Yashoda hysterically described what had happened.

45

A gloom descended over the villagers. They were sure that Krishna would never be found. However, braving the winds, the villagers along with Yashoda and Nanda went in search of Krishna.

They went to the next village and stopped short in front of a cow herd, nestling a perfectly unharmed Krishna in his arms.

"Is this baby yours?" queried the cowherd gently.

Nodding and almost snatching her baby, Yashoda nuzzled Krishna. "How did you find him?" asked Nanda.

"Well, we saw this mass of wind carrying him off. Suddenly, we saw your baby catch the wind. And amazingly, the wind turned into a demon. The baby killed the demon right before our eyes."

Yes, the demon Krishna killed was Trinavarta. He had been sent by Kansa.

Yashoda and Nanda thanked the cowherd and carried Krishna home. However, they found it hard to believe that their podgy baby could have killed a demon!

Krishna, the Miracle Baby

Once, to punish Krishna for his mischief, Yashoda tied him to a massive mortar. Then she went inside the house to do some work. Krishna sat down on his knees and caused the mortar to tumble down so that it could roll when drawn. Then, Krishna began to crawl and the mortar started rolling and got stuck between two trees.

Krishna tugged and pulled the mortar, which made the trees come crashing down. Hearing the loud noise, Yashoda rushed to him. She untied her son clasping him to her bosom, relieved that he had come to no harm.

The twin trees were, in fact, the two sons of Kubera, the God of Wealth. It was because of a curse that they had been turned into trees. When the trees got uprooted, the curse ended, freeing the sons of Kubera from the curse.

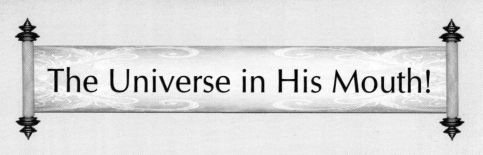

The Universe in His Mouth!

One day, Yashoda spotted Krishna eating a lump of mud. "No, that is unhealthy!" Yashoda rebuked as she stared into Krishna's mouth to scoop out the lump with her fingers. Peering into his mouth, she saw millions of stars, moons and suns; she saw timeless life. Around her astonished eyes, revolved worlds, the entire cosmos; making her feel like a speck in the pattern of existence.

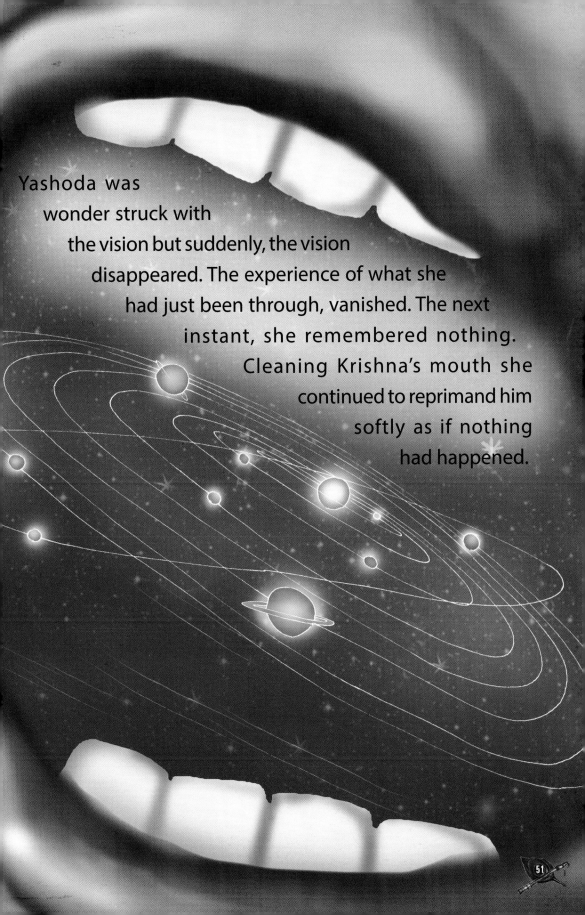

Yashoda was
wonder struck with
the vision but suddenly, the vision
disappeared. The experience of what she
had just been through, vanished. The next
instant, she remembered nothing.
Cleaning Krishna's mouth she
continued to reprimand him
softly as if nothing
had happened.

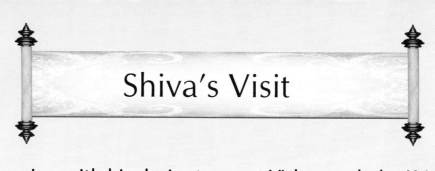

Shiva's Visit

In keeping with his desire to meet Vishnu as baby Krishna, Shiva made his way to Gokul, but not before disguising himself as an ascetic. By intuition, he found his way through the narrow lanes, to the door of Nanda and Yashoda.

"Alms!" Shiva appealed, knocking on the door.

"Wait!" a lady's voice called. In a short while, a charming young woman came into view, carrying a plate full of *laddoos* (sweets).

"For you Baba," said Yashoda, emptying the plate into the ascetic's lap.

"So, you are the new mother?"

"Yes Baba."

"How is the little one?" asked Shiva, glancing over her shoulders, to catch a glimpse of the new baby.

"He is adorable. His name is Krishna," Yashoda proudly glowed.

"Bless him! Can I see the baby?"

The Baba's eagerness to see the baby, made Yashoda uneasy. So she made excuses, "Baba, he is resting. He will cry if I wake him up."

"Just one glimpse," insisted Shiva.

Yashoda shook her head firmly, "No. You cannot meet my baby. Thank you for your blessings, Baba. Now leave!"

"I'd like to bless the child," the disguised Shiva stuck to his demand.

Yashoda coldly rebuffed the Baba, "Forgive my insolence, but I show only pleasant things to my child. Look at you, rough matted hair, ash colouring your skin, filthy attire and those horrible looking beads round your neck. How frightening? My child will get scared if he looks at you." Shiva did not budge. Closing his eyes, he mentally communicated with Vishnu, who was actually lying in the cradle as Krishna. Promptly, there was a loud wailing sound from indoors.

Excuse me!" muttered Yashoda, running indoors.

The baby's wailing intermingled with Yashoda's cajoling. She clutched little Krishna against her shoulder.

"Hush baby," she patted him, pacing up and down. Krishna did not stop crying. Yashoda was frantic. Comforting the crying infant, she stepped out into the courtyard.

Shiva smiled when he laid eyes on Krishna. The moment the child spotted the ascetic, he stopped crying instantly. Instead, baby Krishna began to gurgle happily! Yashoda was astonished. She gazed in awe, as Shiva, in the guise of an ascetic, joined his palms together, then bowed and departed.

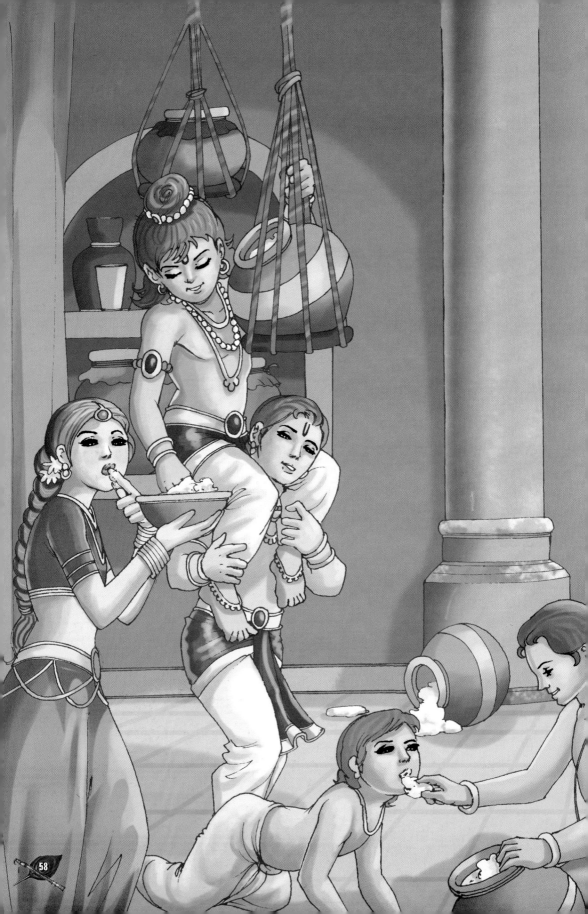

Radha & Krishna

Krishna's favourite playmate was Balaram, Rohini's son. However, they had many other friends too, including a teenage girl called Radha. Radha was from the neighbouring village of Barsana. She did not have a mother. But her father had several wives, giving Radha many step mothers. Radha was considered wild. In fact, she always escaped from her own village and ran to be at the adjoining village of Gokul to be with Krishna. Radha loved to play with Krishna. She spent endless hours singing and chatting with him. Krishna too loved her company. It was not surprising to see Krishna straddled on Radha's hips as she roamed about. Yashoda welcomed Radha's help. As Krishna grew, he, along with Radha, Balaram and a pack of village children, would gang up to play pranks on everyone. Even though Radha was older than all, she was accepted in their group. Their cherished prank was stealing butter from the hanging pot in every hut of the village.

As soon as everyone left for work, Krishna and his gang would sneak in and steal butter.

One day, they even made a human pyramid to reach the pot of butter hanging from the rafters of the hut's roof. One wrong move and they all fell, breaking the pot and soaking themselves in butter!

The villagers were ready to forgive Krishna and his gang anything, but were wary of Radha.

"She is a grown up girl, but how childishly she behaves; tagging after children and joining in their pranks?" they whispered disapprovingly. Radha did not care about the wagging tongues. She loved to be around young Krishna all the time.

It was Radha who fashioned a flute for Krishna when he was young and taught him to play the sweetest tunes on it. However, the other children soon became irritated of Radha's attachment to Krishna. Many a times, Radha and Krishna would go off to play on their own, much to the chagrin of the others. They would trace the two, only to find Krishna playing his flute and Radha sitting by his feet, looking up with rapt attention.

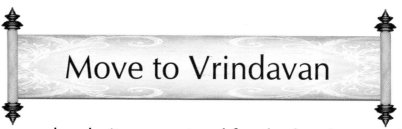

Move to Vrindavan

Being cowherds, it was natural for the herdsmen of Gokul to seek greener pastures for their cattle. There was also the constant harassment caused by one or the other visits of Kansa's evil envoys.

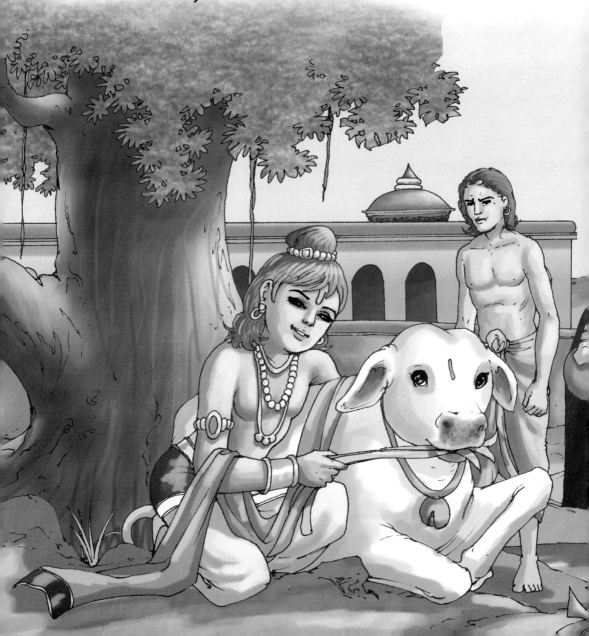

Shortly, the people of Gokul decided to leave their village and settle in the lush pastures of Vrindavan on the banks of the river Yamuna.

Once at Vrindavan, the families from Gokul settled in quickly. So did Krishna's family, as well as Rohini and Balaram amongst others. Radha too made her way there.

The community already living at Vrindavan welcomed these migrants from Gokul.

Krishna adapted quickly to life at his new home. He took his little calves to graze with the other boys. On these trips, Krishna loved to tease the giggling milkmaids carrying urns of milk to the city of Mathura from Vrindavan.

Sometimes he caused chaos by running away with their clothes when they bathed by the river. However, whatever Krishna did, he was forgiven as he was everyone's favourite.

Radha, once, stuck a peacock feather in Krishna's head. Krishna, as he stood cross legged playing his flute, with the feather on his head, represented a beautiful picture, much to the delight of onlookers.

Kaliya

Life in Vrindavan was peaceful. But soon, a problem presented itself. Residing within the river Yamuna, an extremely poisonous cobra, called Kalia, began to trouble the people of Vrindavan. This Cobra had 101 hoods (heads).

His venom poisoned the waters of the Yamuna killing most fish. Even the cattle and the people who drank the poisonous water died instantly. Clouds of gloom and fear covered Vrindavan. The people were no longer happy and children were forbidden to go near the Yamuna river, putting an end to all their merry sport in the cool waters. Krishna decided to kill Kaliya and end the reign of terror. One day, Krishna, while playing with his friends, purposely threw his ball into the poisonous river. Then, he jumped into the waters to get the ball. Kaliya saw Krishna and got furious. Hissing violently, it coiled itself around Krishna. Undaunted, Krishna freed himself from Kaliya's grip and jumped on his hoods. Krishna began to dance on the hoods of the cobra and at the same time began to play on his flute. He laughed as Kaliya tried to shake him off. Then, Krishna stomped his foot so hard on his hood that it got injured and blood started coming out.

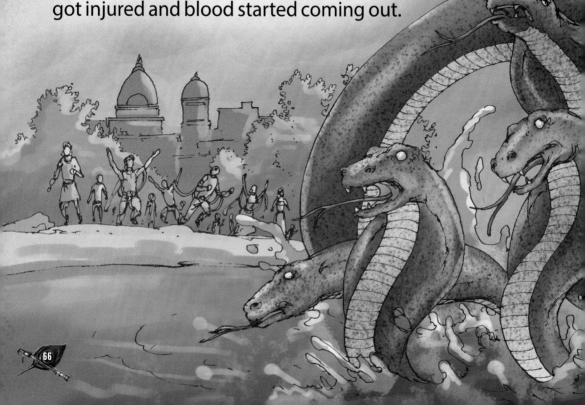

The waters of Yamuna became red as Kaliya's blood mixed with the river water. Seeing the blood, the people on the bank feared the worst; Kaliya would kill Krishna.

But, then, they heard Kaliya's cry for forgiveness,

"Spare me, please spare me," cried Kaliya.

Kaliya's wives too begged Krishna for forgiveness.

"I will spare you," said Krishna, "provided you take your family and go away from here."

Kaliya promised to leave with his family and Krishna leapt off the snake's head.

Kaliya left with his family as promised.
He went to live in the great ocean
far away and never came back
to Vrindavan.

Vaka, the Wizard

Kansa's spies carried tales of Krishna's enchanting presence at Vrindavan, filling him with rage. Especially knowing that Balaram, who he suspected to be Devaki's seventh unborn child, (transferred to Rohini's womb to be born as her child), was alive and a close playmate of Krishna.

"Arrrgh!" he moaned, "how their presence mocks me," Kansa stormed. Kansa called for Vaka, a wizard who had the power to change forms.

"Vaka," ordered Kansa, "go to Vrindavan and kill Krishna."

Vaka reached Vrindavan and intoned a spell, by which he was transformed into a huge wren (bird). Positioning himself on the marshy banks, he slyly waited. Soon, the children collected to view the huge bird. Foremost was Krishna, who gingerly extended his hand to pat the bird. In a loud horrific groan, the bird opened his beak and caught Krishna.

Before he could react, Vaka, disguised as the bird, rose to the sky. Krishna struggled to free himself. With utmost strength, Krishna held the bird's beak and pried it open.

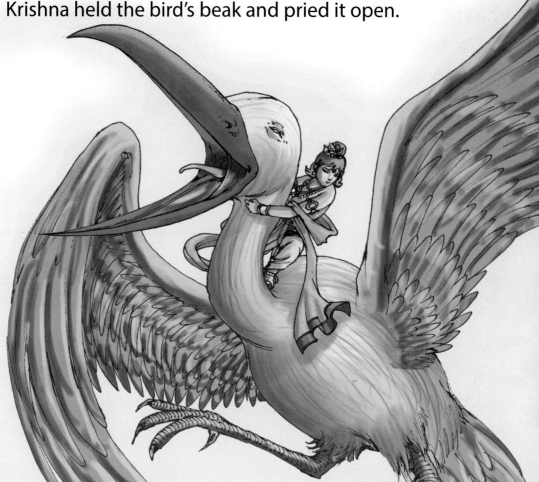

In one simultaneous movement, even as the bird soared higher in the sky, he managed to maneuver deftly, to climb and reach its back. Curving his hands around the bird's neck, Krishna began to throttle it. Vaka had no chance. He fell in a heap from the skies, as Krishna strangled him to death.

Vaka's corpse changed to its true form, from a wren to the wizard he actually was.

Krishna landed unscathed atop the dead wizard, amidst much applause from the relieved citizens of Vrindavan.

Radha gets Married

Radha's father, shaken by the gossip mongers, accusing his daughter to be wild, decided to marry her off. He chose an elderly but rich man from another town for her. Soon, the wedding plans were announced and Vrindavan was filled with anticipation of her wedding. Radha made a beautiful bride. Krishna played the flute throughout her wedding rituals.

Through Krishna's tunes Radha received the message which said, "Radha, you may be leaving us to go into another household, but you will always remain in my heart. No one can separate us!"

Krishna Kills the Python

Yet again, Kansa made an attempt to kill Krishna. This time, he sent a demon, Aghasura, who changed into a huge python and lay on the path along which Krishna and his mates drove their cattle daily. Unknowingly, Krishna's friends, along with their cattle, walked into the mouth of the python, mistaking it for a crack in a hill.

Krishna saw his friends enter the python's mouth and called out, "Stop! You have entered the python's mouth. Turn back and come out!" But his friends could not hear him and continued to walk, straight into the huge reptile's mouth. So, Krishna ran fast and he too got into the python's mouth. Using his powers, Krishna enlarged himself to such a huge size that the python could not close its mouth and devour all of them.

Aghasura now found it difficult to even breathe. Soon, he was chocked to death and Krishna and his friends came out safe and sound.

Krishna & Balaram

Krishna and Balaram, even though they did not know their true relationship yet, were very attached to each other. Krishna had grown into a slender lad, as opposed to Balaram, who was a tall, burly boy. One day, their group of friends unexpectedly discovered a garden hidden in the back waters of Vrindavan. What fascinated them most about this garden was an ancient fig tree.

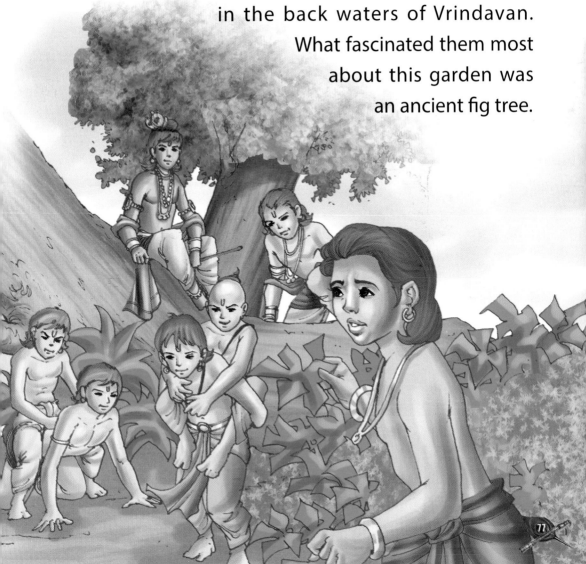

Unfortunately, the boys did not for once suspect that this tree was in reality the home of the demon, Pralamba. "Let us play a game," announced Balaram and Krishna to the others. The game they suggested needed teams, divided into pairs. Unfortunately, one pair fell short. Krishna willingly offered not to play since he did not have a partner. As the game was starting, suddenly, from nowhere, a young boy, seemingly a cowherd, appeared.

"Will you play with us?" Krishna asked.

"Yes," said the boy.

This way, Krishna found his partner and he too joined the game. After an hour of noise, hooting and claps, the game finished with the victors being lifted by the losers on their shoulders. Balaram was heaved up by the new boy, whom he had defeated. "Hey stop! Why are you running off with me still on your shoulders?" Balaram yelled.

But the stranger just ran. To his horror Balaram saw the boy transforming into an ugly demon. This demon was Pralamba. He had disguised himself to join the group of children playing so he could choose one of them to eat. He chose Balaram as he seemed to be the fattest. Succeeding in his schemes, Pralamba now carried Balaram off. Scared witless, Balaram squealed, "Help me, Krishna…help!"

Without being seen, Krishna seemed to engulf Balaram with his presence.

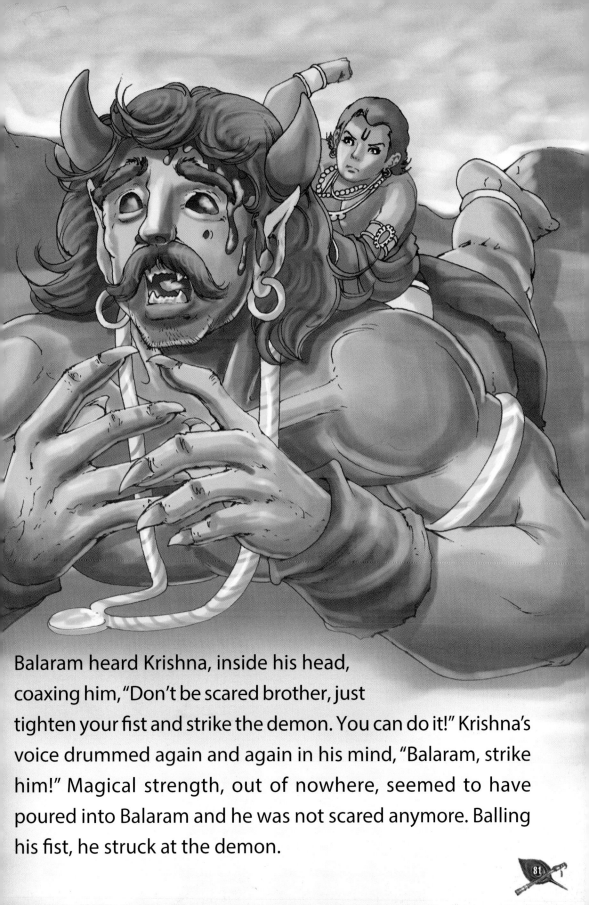

Balaram heard Krishna, inside his head, coaxing him, "Don't be scared brother, just tighten your fist and strike the demon. You can do it!" Krishna's voice drummed again and again in his mind, "Balaram, strike him!" Magical strength, out of nowhere, seemed to have poured into Balaram and he was not scared anymore. Balling his fist, he struck at the demon.

"Arrrg!" the demon breathlessly tumbled to the ground. Hastily, getting to his feet, Balaram punched the demon once more. The demon gave out a horrible shriek and fell down dead. Balaram looked around to see where Krishna was and was bewildered when he realized that he was alone, save for the dead demon. He could have sworn that Krishna had helped him! By now, his friends and Krishna had reached him. Balaram was confused. Even as everyone applauded him for killing the demon, Balaram kept looking at Krishna suspiciously. Krishna, with a mysterious smile, stood in one corner, saying nothing.

Balaram & Dhenuka

Balaram became quite a hero for killing Pralamba. Balaram, however, once again found himself in a precarious situation. Inadvertently, Balaram wandered into the beetel nut palm tree grove. This area was avoided because wild asses stayed here. Anyone venturing close would actually be kicked to death by them. Dhenuka was the king of these asses. Balaram realized his folly when he was picking up beetel nuts and he heard the savage brays of the vexed asses.

Rooted to the spot, Balaram's heart sank as he recognized the danger he was in. The growling asses were slowly surrounding him. Their king, Dhenuka, began the offensive by lunging at him with a blood curdling scream. But Balaram was waiting for him! Grasping Dhenuka by his hind legs Balaram began to swing him around, revolving round and round. Horrified, Balaram, over his shoulders saw the other asses, closing in on him with murderous intent.

"Krishna!" Balaram screamed. Magically, Krishna was besides him. The brothers in unison tackled the attack. It was not long before all the asses were dead and the beetel nut palm tree grove became safe for everyone once more.

Indra's Ire

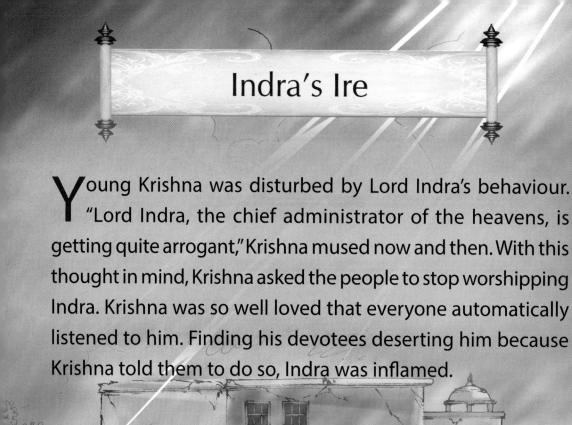

Young Krishna was disturbed by Lord Indra's behaviour. "Lord Indra, the chief administrator of the heavens, is getting quite arrogant," Krishna mused now and then. With this thought in mind, Krishna asked the people to stop worshipping Indra. Krishna was so well loved that everyone automatically listened to him. Finding his devotees deserting him because Krishna told them to do so, Indra was inflamed.

In his anger, he summoned the black rain clouds and ordered them to rain in a deluge over Vrindavan. The unending heavy rains grew into a natural calamity. The people begged Krishna to help them. Krishna did not let them down. In front of many astonished eyes he lifted *Govardhan Parvat*, the largest mountain in the vicinity, in one heave. He instructed everyone to take cover under the mountain, as he held it up high on his little finger. The entire village found safe haven under the mountain.

Watching from the skies, Indra was dumbfounded. He continued to send storms and rains to Vrindavan. Krishna was unaffected. He stood holding the mountain resolutely and unwavering. The mountain provided excellent cover for everyone. Indra slowly felt a feeling of grudging admiration for Krishna and realized why Krishna had stopped people from praying to him.

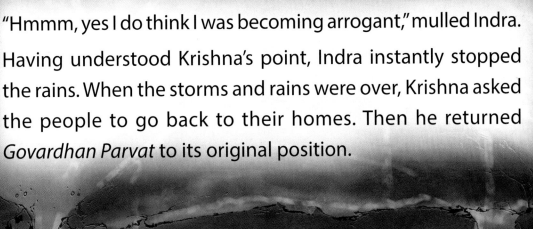

"Hmmm, yes I do think I was becoming arrogant," mulled Indra.

Having understood Krishna's point, Indra instantly stopped the rains. When the storms and rains were over, Krishna asked the people to go back to their homes. Then he returned *Govardhan Parvat* to its original position.

Kansa's Threats

Kansa could not get over his restlessness to kill Krishna. His spies would carry back tales of valour of Krishna and Balaram to him and his heart would burn with anger. "I have to kill these two. They mock me and my strength."

Having said this, Kansa decided to invite everyone for paying their respect to a great bow amongst festivities.

"The mighty bow will be for sacrifice. All subjects of my kingdom will attend to salute this bow. Apart from that, there shall be wrestling matches." His eyes took on an evil gleam and he drawled, "To participate in the wrestling match, I will order Nanda to send his son and nephew too!" An emissary was sent to Gokul and Nanda was instructed to send the boys for a wrestling match. The messenger, however, warned them that Kansa actually meant to kill the boys. "They are to fight with the demons Chunura and Mushtika in a wrestling match. No one has ever defeated these two," the messenger blurted. "I will go," Krishna said. "Me too!" Balaram put in eagerly. Yashoda, Nanda and everyone else could not dissuade the boys. With much reluctance, they bade farewell to them as they left for Mathura.

Rukmi

When the boys entered Mathura, the first thing they noticed was Jarasandha's soldiers milling the place. They also noticed the scared uneasiness amongst the people. A few days before the matches were to begin, Krishna was in the market square, when a commotion arrested his steps. A young man, dressed in princely garbs, rode his chariot relentlessly through the crowded place. He was Rukmi, the powerful ally of Kansa. Rukmi was the son of Bhismaka, king of Vidarbha.

Lashing his whip, he raced his carriage forth, hardly bothered at how he was injuring people. Suddenly, the coach stopped abruptly with a squeal of wheels as Krishna sprang in front. "Out of my way!"
roared Rukmi.

Krishna instantly grabbed Rukmi's whip and waggled it near his face. Rukmi was livid. "You commoner! How dare you do this? Don't you know who I am?"

"I dare do this. Come, let's have a duel to sort things out," Krishna laughed. Almost purple with rage, Rukmi spat, "I don't duel with filthy commoners. Now, out of my way!" snatching his whip, Rukmi walloped his horses forth. As the carriage bounced forward, the curtains at the back blew out because of the wind. Krishna caught sight of a beautiful woman's face peeping out of the carriage window. It was Rukmini, Rukmi's sister. Krishna continued to stare long after the carriage disappeared.

Kubja

Krishna and Balaram were becoming quite popular in Mathura. In fact, in hushed whispers, Krishna's divine miracles were being discussed. One such miracle was when the local deformed, hunchback, a woman called Kubja, came in his presence.

She was shunned by all because of her ugliness but had a rare specialty. She could make the most fragrant of perfumes ever smelled before. Clutching one such vial of perfume, she came in the way of Krishna and Balaram one day. To the astonishment of all, she drew close to Krishna and poured an entire vial of perfume over him. The air filled with a heady aroma. The smell was so divine that most people closed their eyes and took deep breaths. Kubja herself fell to her knees softly chanting, "Krishna-Krishna!" In front of everyone's shocked eyes, Krishna laid her hand over her head and all her deformities disappeared, turning her into a beautiful woman.

The Bow

Finally, the day of the Bow sacrifice came. Confidently, the two brothers entered the palace gates to get to the grounds where this bow was kept on a high stage. Krishna reached the bow. He did not prostrate before it.

A gasp ensued as Krishna lifted the mighty bow easily. Holding each end of the bow, he snapped it into two. The hollow twang of the snapping bow filled the area; a loud applause broke through as everyone clapped uncontrollably seeing the magnificent feat.

When Kansa heard what had happened, he tried to control his tensed mind and ordered,

"Call the wrestlers now."

Chunura and Mushtika looked greedily as Kansa waved precious jewels in front of them.

"These are yours if you finish those two cowherds from Gokul." The wrestlers agreed covetously, their eyes fixed on the loot they hoped to get.

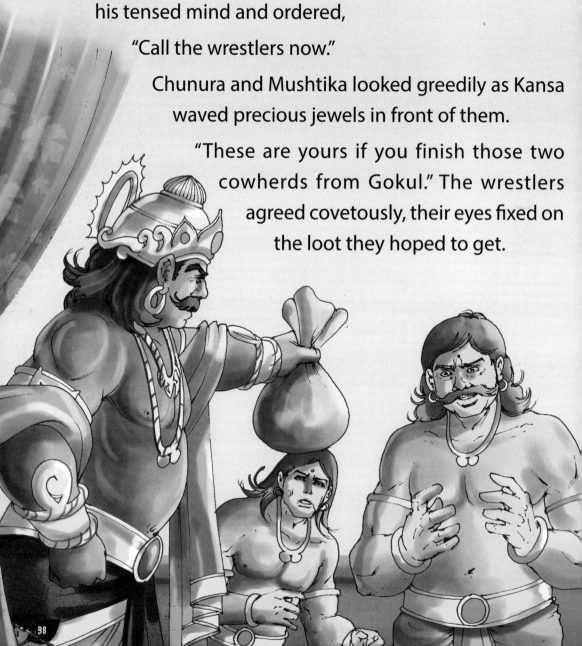

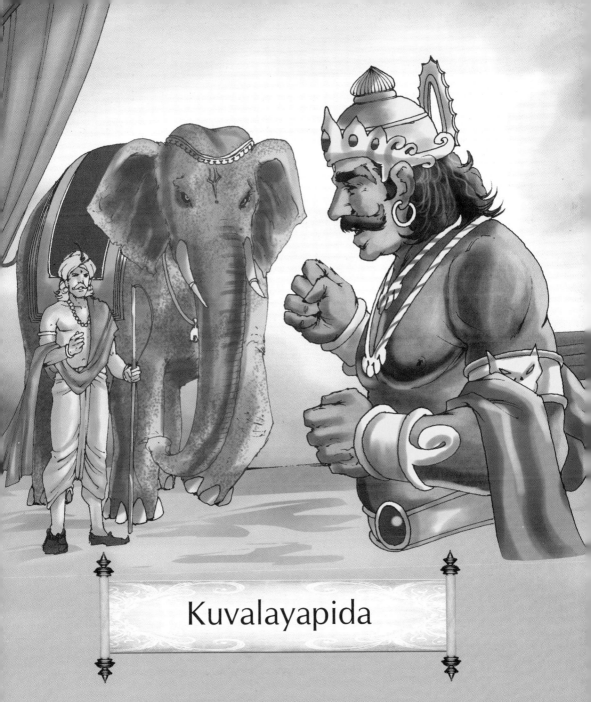

Kuvalayapida

Kansa was still insecure. He decided to keep the wrestlers as a back up. Before that, he instructed his elephant trainer to position Kuvalayapida, the rogue elephant, at the entry gate of the wrestling ring. "But Kuvalayapida hates humans…he will trample any one in his sight to death," gulped the trainer.

Kansa bellowed, "Do as I say or
you shall be hanged." The next
morning, Krishna and Balaram entered the wrestling ring.
"Trummmmmmmp!" Kuvalayapida charged at them. Krishna
stood still, as did his brother. As soon as the elephant reached
them, his anger seemed to have left him. He knelt before
Krishna. Kansa almost fainted with shock when he saw Krishna
and Balaram enter the ring, riding a benign Kuvalayapida.

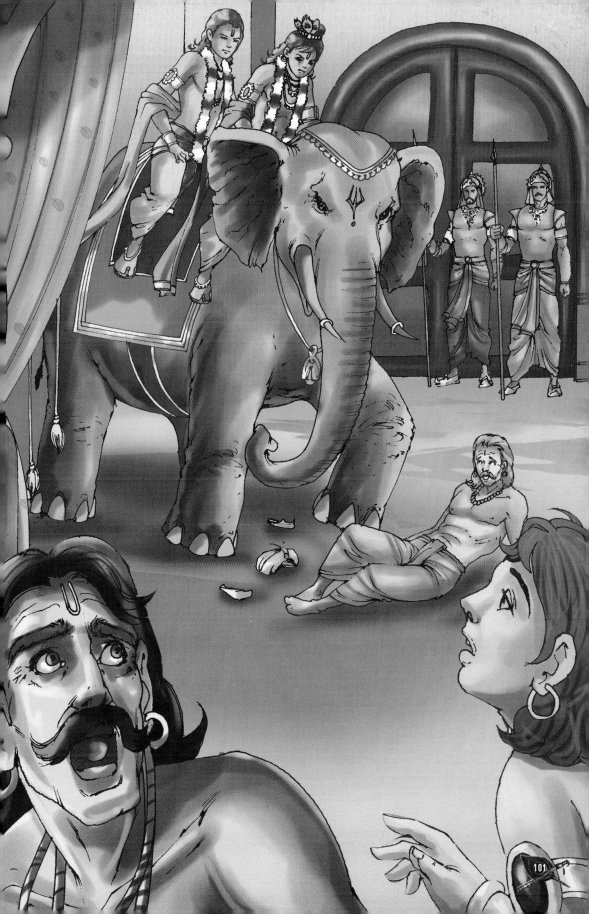

End of Kansa

Triumphantly, Krishna dismounted to wrestle the demon, Chunura. Kansa eagerly sat at the edge of his seat thinking, 'Krishna will meet his end, at last!'

He could not have been more wrong. Chunura was given the thrashing of his life. Finally, Krishna broke his back.

Mushtika met the same fate at the hands of Balaram, who dashed to prevent Mushtika from attacking Krishna, after he had killed Chunura. Balaram twisted this wrestler, killing him instantly. Both the dreaded wrestlers were dead. This event had the crowds beside themselves with joy.

Furious at the obvious support to the two, Kansa ordered his soldiers to arrest Krishna and Balaram.

Chaos ensued. Balaram and Krishna fought off the soldiers.

Then came that moment, which every one was waiting for. Krishna adroitly jumped on to the platform where Kansa sat on his throne. With a cry, Krishna attacked Kansa with a dagger in hand and plunged it under his chest, rendering him dead. Thus, came the end of Kansa's evil rule.

Jarasandha Attacks

Sadly, once the dictator Kansa was vanquished, there was no peace at Mathura. Krishna declined to take the throne, since, legally, he was Kansa's nephew and not his son. Instead, Krishna freed his grandfather Ugrasena, who was old and feeble, and reinstalled him to the throne, by common consensus from the other statesmen of the kingdom.

Krishna and Balaram then stood before their real parents, Devaki and Vasudeva.

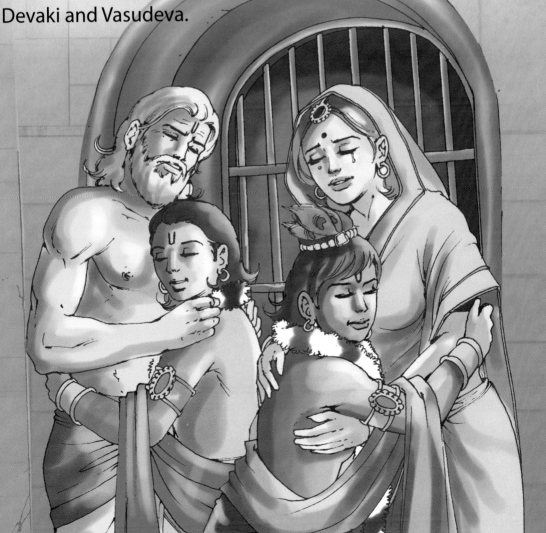

By now, Krishna and Balaram knew the truth about their births. Poignant justice had been served and Devaki and Vasudeva held their sons close; in some way washing away the horrors of the past experiences they had gone through.

Meanwhile, Jarasandha, king of Magadh, who was Kansa's father in law, vowed to attack Mathura and finish the 'two upstart cowherds who had killed his son in law!'

Everyone knew that the actual power behind Kansa's throne was his father in law. Jarasandha was impossible to defeat as he had special powers.

The legend goes that when Jarasandha was born, he had only half a body. His worried parents approached a medicine woman, who by her magical cures, made Jarasandha's body whole again. Jarasandha now had two separate parts of body flimsily joined together. It was said that even if the separate parts of his body broke into two, he could rejoin his body within minutes and rise again. By the powers of the medicine woman, Jarasandha possessed super natural strength and a boon that no weapon could kill him. That is why Jarasandha became so arrogant. He went berserk claiming power and vanquishing kingdoms. It was said that he had captured eighty six kings and thrown them into the prisons of Magadh.

A furious Jarasandha came looking for Krishna and Balaram to Mathura but the two had been whisked away to safety.

Krishna's Education

Krishna and Balaram were sent to the ashram of Sandipani to study the art of war and to learn the Vedas. Sage Sandipani was considered to be one of the greatest teachers of that time. Krishna made a very good friend at the ashram. His name was Sudama. Sudama was a poor Brahmin boy who was also being tutored by Sandipani.

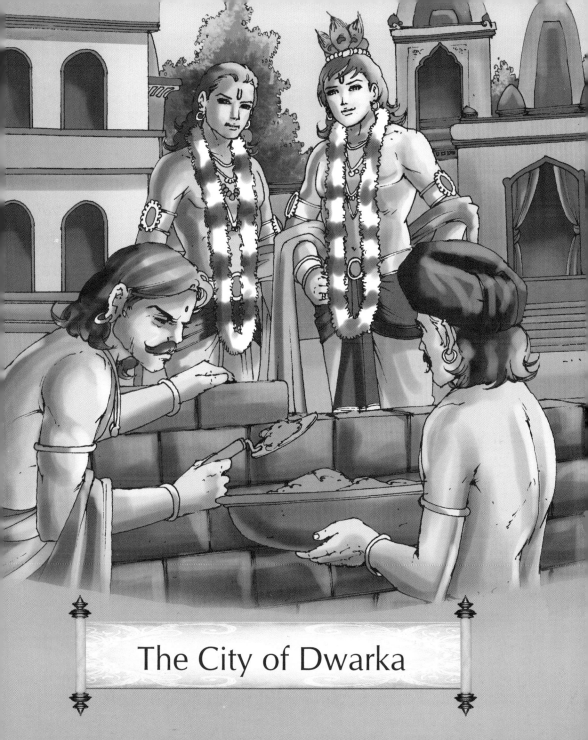

The City of Dwarka

"**K**rishna save us!" cried the harried emissaries from Mathura. "Jarasandha has made our lives hell after Kansa was killed. Now we feel only you can help us out. Come back to Mathura!"

Their pleading had the desired effect and Krishna along with Balaram returned to Mathura. Krishna immediately charted out a plan in order to thwart Jarasandha's attacks. "Build an impregnable wall around the city." Jarasandha found it impossible to break through this wall. He laid siege to the city of Mathura. However, months went by and there was a dead lock. Meanwhile, in the skirmishes, Jarasandha lost two of his best friends.

Disheartened, he decided to lift the siege and retreat. But his retreat held no happiness for Mathura. They knew he would be back. "It would be best if we migrated westward," suggested Krishna. After many discussions, this move was made. A beautiful land by the sea was identified and named Dwarka. Within days, the population of Mathura, with Balaram and Krishna as their leaders, moved to Dwarka. Soon, Dwarka was flourishing under their able rule.

Peace at Dwarka

Dwarka progressed rapidly under the leadership of Balaram and Krishna. However, the two never forgot their exciting days at Gokul and Vrindavan. Krishna always obeyed his elder brother. Meanwhile, Devaki and Vasudeva gave birth to a girl child. She was called Subhadra. Subhadra was under the care of her two brothers who loved her dearly. Seeing her growing into a beautiful maiden they often wondered who the charming prince would be who would marry their lovely sister.

Rukmini

King Bhismaka had a daughter called Rukmini and a son called Rukmi. Rukmini was hopelessly in love with Krishna. On the other hand, her brother Rukmi hated Krishna.

Rukmi's friends were *Jarasandha*, the Emperor of Magadh and *Shishupal*, the King of Chedi. Rukmi had also been friends with Kansa and the death of Kansa by Krishna, enraged Rukmi.

He wanted his sister, Rukmini, to marry Shishupal.

Rukmini came to know of her brother's intentions and decided to write to Krishna.

Her letter was smuggled out by a Brahmin messenger. When Krishna read the letter, he smiled and immediately fell in love with this brave damsel. Krishna gave a verbal reply,

"Tell Rukmini to come to the temple before her marriage rites. I will be waiting there for her. No force on earth can stop me, now that I know she loves me so much!"

Rukmini was thrilled when she received the reply. Secretly, Rukmini knew Krishna would save her. So, she behaved normally, not raising any suspicions.

Splendour and pomp marked the wedding day. Rukmini came out from the temple and her eyes wandered about, but she could not see her beloved Krishna.

"Come, let's go my lovely," someone laughed into her ear as a firm hand curved around her waist and she was lifted on to a chariot.

"*Krishna!*" said Rukmini excitedly. "Away, we go!" Krishna chuckled, whipping his horses to move fast. Her brother, Rukmi, realizing what had happened, roared,

"Stop them!"

A chase ensued. Meanwhile at Dwarka, Krishna's brother Balaram was told of Krishna's plan of elopement with Rukmini. He decided to meet Krishna with an army.

"Things can turn ugly and he might need my help," Balaram pondered. On the other side, Jarasandha too, hotly tailed Krishna. Dodging all, Krishna sailed through the gates of Dwarka. Seeing Krishna safe, Balaram immediately pushed Jarasandha's army away! Rukmi, however, sped through the gates, closely following Krishna. Krishna released his arrows and shattered the wheels of Rukmi's chariot, toppling it. Rukmi stumbled and fell at Krishna's feet.

Krishna was about to behead him but Rukmini begged him to spare her brother's life! Krishna agreed. Krishna lifted Rukmini and took her into Dwarka. The inhabitants were overjoyed. The couple were married in a grand affair.

Satyabhama

Oone day, a man by the name of Satrajit lost a very precious jewel given to him by the Sun God. Not able to find it, a distraught Satrajit included Krishna in his list of suspects. Satrajit did not trust Krishna. Actually, the jewel had been found by a monster named Jambavat who lived inside a dark cave in the deep forests. No one suspected that he had the jewel.

However, soon people began to gossip hinting Krishna may have stolen it. To allay these rumours, Krishna began to search for the jewel. His search led him to Jambavat's cave. Krishna challenged him to a battle which Jambavat agreed to. For twenty eight days, they fought inside the cave. Finally, Krishna killed the monster and triumphantly returned the jewel to a sheepish Satrajit who was ashamed at accusing him thus. Shortly after this incident, Satrajit's daughter, Satyabhama, was married to Krishna. Along with Rukmini, Satyabhama stayed at the palace in Dwarka as Krishna's second wife.

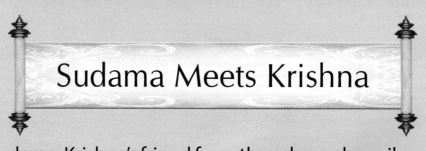

Sudama Meets Krishna

Sudama, Krishna's friend from the ashram, happily received news of his friend's glory.

"Why don't you go and ask Krishna for help?" his wife archly asked when for the umpteenth time Sudama related one tale or the other of their friendship.

"We can do with some help, you know?" she further added, pointing to their thread bare clothes and obvious poverty.

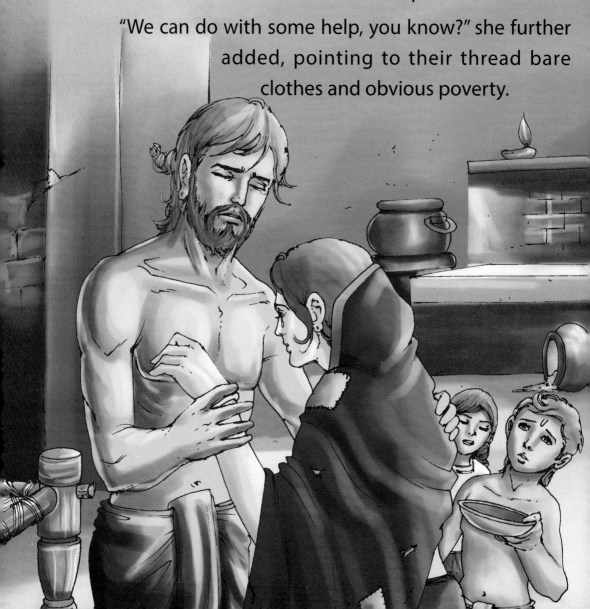

Urged constantly by his wife, to renew his connection with Krishna and ask for help to get them out of their poor conditions, Sudama decided to visit his friend. Carrying a small pouch of puffed rice, he reached the palace gates. Krishna was overjoyed to see Sudama. On the other hand, Sudama was bewildered by the magnificence of Dwarka palace. He could not utter a word. Krishna accepted his present of puffed rice and they sat for a while. Later, Sudama made his way back home with the heavy thought, 'I forgot to ask Krishna for help.'

But Sudama got a pleasant surprise when he
reached his impoverished hut. Instead
of his humble hut, stood a beautiful
house with a stocked granary!
His wife had clothes and money.
Sudama wept gratefully thinking
that his friend was truly the best.

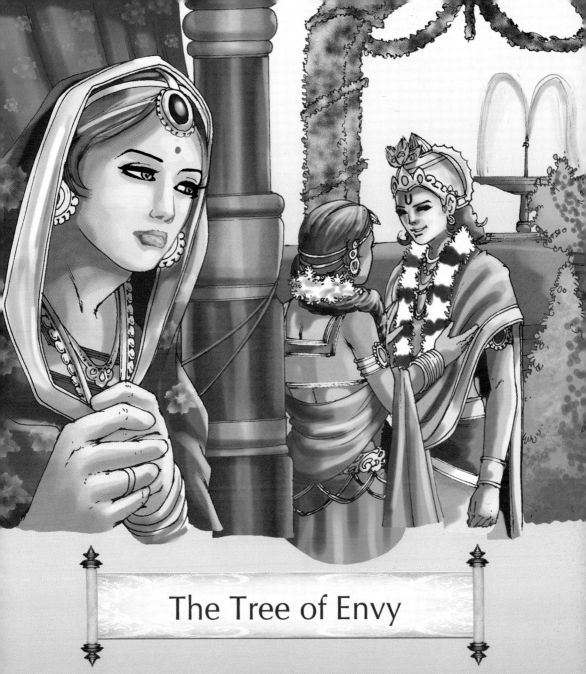

The Tree of Envy

Satyabhama watched with envy as Rukmini made a garland of flowers from the Parijata tree that grew in the garden on her side of the palace. "She gathers flowers and gives Krishna a garland everyday!" fumed Satyabhama.

One day, she complained to Krishna asking him for a Parijata tree too.

"It seems you love Rukmini more, she has this tree and I don't," Satyabhama playfully reproached Krishna. Instantly, Krishna offered to help her grow this tree on her side of the fence.

Krishna chose the spot where he helped her plant the sapling of the tree. Diligently, the two nurtured the tree. The tree grew big and flowered beautifully. Satyabhama was initially happy to see the tree but later she was in for a rude shock. Her tree had flowered but it had grown in such a way that it leaned over the fence into Rukmini's palace garden and threw all its flowers there! Therefore, Rukmini's garden was strewn with flowers from Satyabhama's tree! Hearing Krishna chuckling, Satyabhama too laughed, forgetting about her grouse and enjoying the joke with her husband!

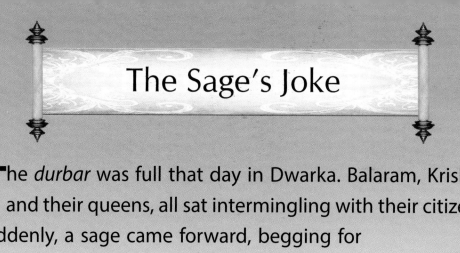

The Sage's Joke

The *durbar* was full that day in Dwarka. Balaram, Krishna and their queens, all sat intermingling with their citizens. Suddenly, a sage came forward, begging for alms. "You may have as much gold as you want," Balaram declared seeing how poor the man was.

"I would like to have the gold equivalent to Krishna's weight. If you cannot find that much of gold, then I want Krishna himself," stated the sage seriously. Affronted that the sage thought Dwarka did not have so much of gold, the royals agreed to his condition to prove him wrong. Huge weights were brought. Krishna sat on one side. Gold was piled on to the other. Oh dear, all the amount of gold, precious treasures and the wealth of Dwarka could not equal Krishna's weight.

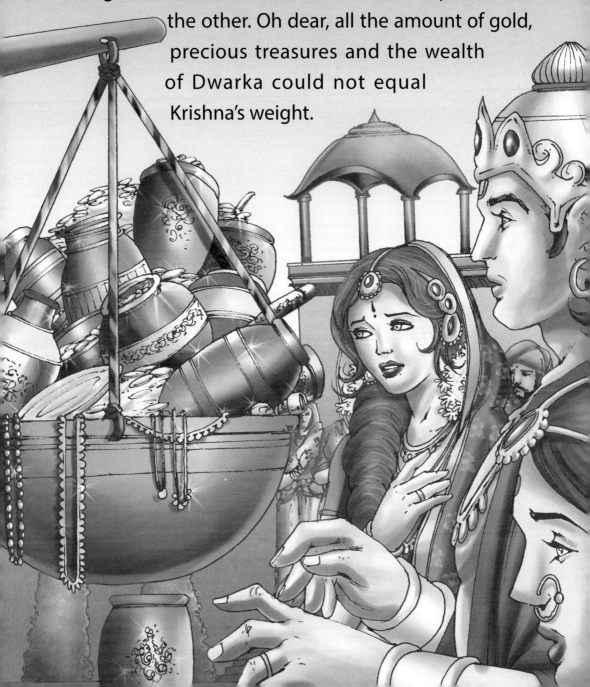

"Oh no! We will have to give Krishna to this sage," sobbed Satyabhama.

Meanwhile, Rukmini stared hard at the sage. She suddenly smiled. "Wait!" she ran inside and plucked a leaf of the holy *tulsi* plant. This was Krishna's favourite herb.

Rukmini had all the treasures removed from the scales, although she requested Krishna to keep sitting. Then, with a twinkle in her eyes, she dropped the sprig of tulsi on the scale! Suddenly, the scales showed the *tulsi* sprig weighing exactly as much as Krishna! Now, how Rukmini had gathered that this sage was none other than the heavenly messenger, Narada; no one really knows. Some say she caught his lips twitching. Others say she caught the deep look Krishna and he exchanged; all the same her ploy worked. Laughing, the sage picked up the sprig of *tulsi* and walked away.

Krishna & the Pandavas

King Drupada of Panchala held a *swayamwara* for his daughter, Draupadi. Kings from all over were invited. Balaram and Krishna too were present. Out of the blue, five Brahmins entered and sat with the other hopeful grooms. When everyone was seated, King Drupada said, "I have set a test. The man who wins the test marries my daughter. Near the pool, there is a bow. Directly overhead on the ceiling is a golden fish revolving at high speed. The man who wants to marry my daughter, must first string the bow and then hit the eye of the fish with one arrow. This he must do by looking at its reflection in the water."

The kings tensed on hearing this; this was not going to be easy. One by one, they rose and tried to bend the bow but not one of them could even string it. It was one of the Brahmins who rose and succeeded in the task. This Brahmin was Arjun, one of the five Pandavas, sons of king Pandu and Kunti from the kingdom of Hastinapur.

Unfortunately, after King Pandu died, the Pandava brothers, and their mother Kunti, were driven out from their kingdom by their jealous cousin, Duryodhana. They were denied their rightful inheritance also.

Duryodhana belonged to the ruling Kaurava clan. He had a hundred brothers. In a bid to kill the Pandavas, Duryodhana had set their palace ablaze. Luckily, the Pandavas escaped unscathed. However, no one knew they were alive, except Krishna. "What sort of Brahmins were these?" Balaram asked Krishna. Krishna looked highly amused at how the Pandavas had fooled the entire court of Drupada with their disguise of Brahmins. "It is obvious that they are the five Pandavas," he whispered to his brother. "How can that be? The Pandava brothers are dead!" replied Balaram confidently.

"It is them. Now things are going to move in full motion. You wait and watch!" Krishna drawled to a thoughtful Balaram.

After daring to win princess Draupadi, the Pandavas went home. When the Pandavas entered their hut in the forest, Kunti, who was busy with some chore, didn't turn around.

"Look at what I got for alms today, mother," Arjun said with a laugh. "Share it equally among yourselves," Kunti said and then turned to face them. Her eyes widened in dismay when she saw Draupadi beside Arjun.

"Oh, what have I done!" she exclaimed. "Yet, what I have said can't be taken back."

The Pandavas had never disobeyed their mother and neither could they do it then. Yudhishthira, the eldest of the Pandava brothers, bowed and said, "We will obey you as always, mother."

Thus, Draupadi became the wife of all the five brothers.

Jarasandha is Killed

Political storms were brewing over Hastinapur. In a cunning move, Duryodhana's father, Dhritrashtra, who was blind, gave the Pandavas a barren land to claim as their kingdom; a move to appease their demand for their rightful inheritance. Accepting the land without protest, the Pandavas made a paradise out of it, much to the envy of the Kauravas, especially Duryodhana.

They called it Indraprastha. Consequently, Krishna had become a very close friend and confidante of the Pandavas. Yudhishthira, the eldest Pandava, ruled Indraprastha. Yudhishthira expressed a desire to be declared emperor of the entire realm. However, he needed to perform the Rajasuya Yagna for that. He also needed complete control of all kingdoms, unopposed by anyone, to his credit, before he could begin the Yagna.

This wish of Yudhishthira was discussed amongst the Pandavas. When these discussions were taking place, Krishna was present too. Krishna brought to everyone's attention the fact that the tyrant ruler, King Jarasandha, who Krishna himself was fighting, would fiercely oppose this claim of Yudhishthira. It was not easy to depose Jarasandha though. He had a special gift as we have read earlier and killing him was not easy. After much planning, Bhima, Arjun and Krishna decided to meet Jarasandha and challenge him. They disguised themselves as wandering Brahmins and reached the city of Magadh to perform prayers for his welfare.

With scores of other Brahmins invited to perform special prayers, the three also arrived at the royal court. When Jarasandha looked closer, he recognized Bhima, Arjun and Krishna. Krishna said on being discovered, "Yes, we are not Brahmins. You have recognized us correctly. Jarasandha, we have come to challenge you to a duel." Highly amused, Jarasandha rubbed his hands and said discerningly, "I will only duel with the strongest of the three. I choose to fight Bhima, who is just about equal to me in strength." Having said that, an arena was prepared and Bhima and Jarasandha began to wrestle. The fight went on for days.

However, there came a moment when Jarasandha slipped. Grabbing the chance, Bhima rolled him over and effortlessly snapped his body into two halves. Flinging the parts away, Bhima raised his hands in victory and ran towards Arjun and Krishna. Oh dear, right behind him, the two parts of Jarasandha crawled towards each other and joined up! Instantly, Jarasandha stood again. The duel continued. Again days flew, but the wrestling continued. Jarasandha seemed to have more strength then ever. Bhima was tiring. One day, his eyes wandered to Krishna, even though his limbs were locked in a deadly embrace with Jarasandha. Krishna saw him, nodded, then did a strange thing. He bent and picked up a twig. Raising the twig he broke it into two.

Then he crossed his hands over his chest, and threw the twig pieces over his shoulders.

This way, the piece in his right hand flew to the left and the twig in his left hand flew to the right!

Bhima immediately understood the tactic. In a rush of strength, he battered Jarasandha and gained an advantage. With a roar, he raised Jarasandha's body.

He placed it over his knee; once again snapped it into two halves; crossed his hands and flung the halves over his shoulders. Now both the parts were at opposites of each other! The more they crawled to join together, the more they moved further away.

That is how Jarasandha was killed.

The captured princes were freed and Yudhishthira prepared for doing the Rajasuya Yagna peacefully.

Krishna Beheads Shishupal

The Rajasuya Yagna was nearing completion. The last act was to confer honours upon the kings who had participated in the ritual. Before starting this rite, it was customary to worship the best participant. For this, Krishna's name was proposed. Most of the kings seconded the proposal but Shishupal and his supporters, opposed it. Shishupal had an old grudge against Krishna. He opposed the worship of Krishna as the best participant using objectionable and disgraceful words for him.

Krishna stood up and addressed the gathering, "I beg the attention of all of you to what I am going to say. Shishupal is my cousin, son of my father's sister. I would have done away with him far earlier but for his mother's request to pardon him.

Now I warn him to come to the right path. I won't say or do anything till he has used at least one hundred disgraceful terms for me. But after that, I won't spare him at all." Shishupal, not heeding Krishna's words, continued his abusive barrage of words. Finally, after Shishupal had abused Krishna a hundred times, Krishna warned, "Shishupal, you have abused me hundred times; now if you say another abusive word, then I will not spare you." Shishupal laughed on hearing this and continued his verbal abuse. The next moment, Lord Vishnu's divine weapon, the *chakra*, appeared in Krishna's hand. Krishna wielded his *chakra* and directed it towards Shishupal. The *chakra*, revolving, went towards Shishupal and severed his head from the rest of his body.

The Game of Dice

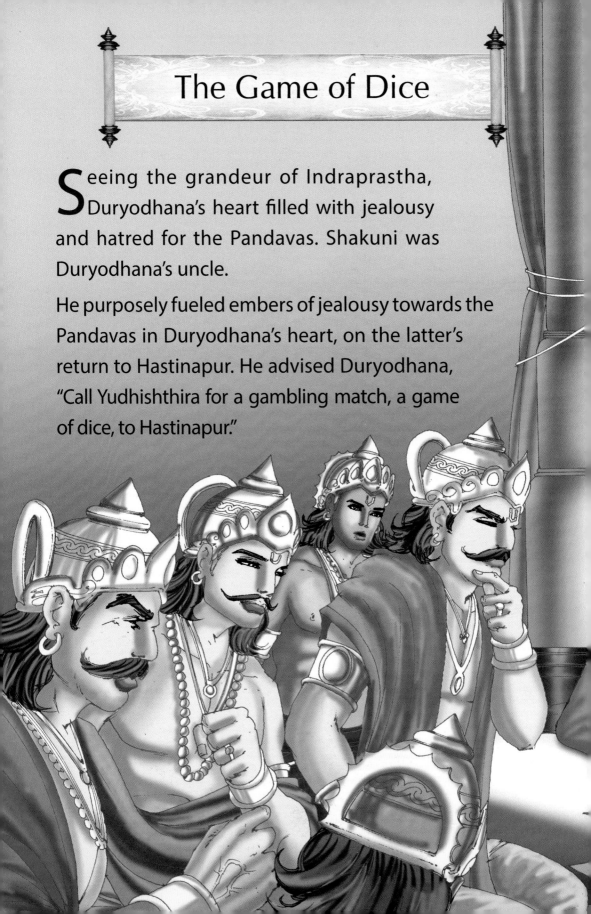

Seeing the grandeur of Indraprastha, Duryodhana's heart filled with jealousy and hatred for the Pandavas. Shakuni was Duryodhana's uncle.

He purposely fueled embers of jealousy towards the Pandavas in Duryodhana's heart, on the latter's return to Hastinapur. He advised Duryodhana, "Call Yudhishthira for a gambling match, a game of dice, to Hastinapur."

"Every one knows Yudhishthira has sworn off gambling. He used to be a gambler, but now is not," dismissed Duryodhana. "Nephew, think! Can a gambler ever leave gambling?" A slow smile dawned over Duryodhana's face. Knowing he had driven his point home, Shakuni drew closer, shuffling and rubbing the dice. "I will defeat him, nephew… just invite him to the gambling boards. Then watch what I do."

Just as predicted, Yudhishthira could not resist this challenge. To his mind, it seemed to be rude to refuse an invitation from his cousin. Duryodhana greeted the Pandavas heartily on their arrival. Yudhishthira came to Hastinapur, accompanied by his brothers and wife Draupadi. The *durbar* was full. Stately courtiers lined the viewing circles. A clear indication, from a noble, signaled the start of the game. But when they sat to play, Yudhishthira questioned the presence of Shakuni, "You and I, Duryodhana, were supposed to play. Then how come your uncle plays instead of you?" Duryodhana's tone took on a teasing inflection, "Are you worried of playing with a better player?" Of course, Yudhishthira did not protest after that. No Kshatriya worth his lineage ever admitted that he could not take a challenge.

But as the game progressed, Yudhishthira began to lose heavily. Shakuni cheated so cleverly that Yudhishthira had no chance. Eventually, Yudhisthira lost everything. His palace, his treasuries and Indraprastha. Still he continued to play.

Yudhishthira was so struck by the gambling bug that he could not discontinue playing! Further goaded by Duryodhana, he bet all his brothers and wife Draupadi, and lost them all.

"Ha, ha! You Pandavas are all my slaves," laughed Duryodhana.

"Bring that queen of yours, Draupadi. Bring Draupadi," roared Duryodhana.

The elders rose to object. A hum of opposing voices erupted.

Dhritrashtra's thin voice joined their babble too. Duryodhana was not listening,

"Call Draupadi!" he screamed.

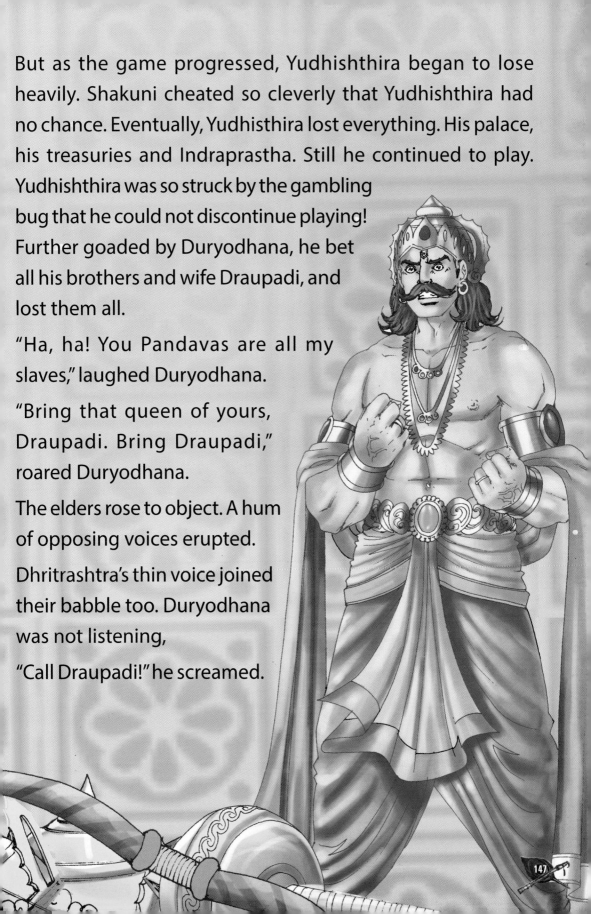

147

"Krishna," She Called!

Duryodhana sent his brother Dushasana to call Draupadi. Draupadi vehemently refused to go. Dushasana chased her and inspite of her violent protests, dragged her into the centre of the *durbar* and left her there, to stand like an exhibit. Draupadi straightened herself, and in a clear voice, reprimanded all for being party to such dreadful deeds.

Angered by her arrogance, Duryodhana, mad with triumph, ordered his brother to strip Draupadi.

'That should bring her pride down,' thought Duryodhana.

Knowing no one could help her, Draupadi closed her eyes and began to pray to Lord Krishna.

"Krishna-Krishna, help me dear Lord! Help me," she chanted.

The Pandava brothers helplessly beheld this appalling suffering their wife was put through. They were Duryodhana's slaves, having been gambled away by Yudhishthira, and were bound by a discipline they could not break. Dushasana lunged and pulled Draupadi's *saree* by one end. "*Krishna!* Oh Lord, save me," Draupadi cried into her hands.

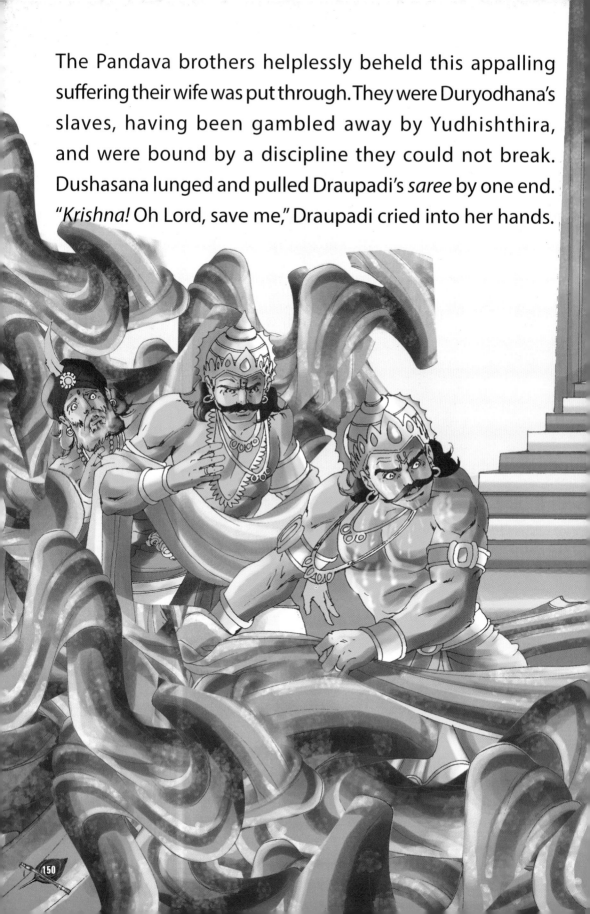

Unseen by all, a splinter of light cracked a trail, splitting into millions of sequins and invisibly wrapped itself over the beleaguered Draupadi. Lord Krishna had heard her prayers! Dushasana noticed nothing. He continued to yank the saree in order to strip Draupadi. *But the length of her saree just would not finish!* Her saree began to grow longer and longer! Dushasana reeled off the *saree* endlessly but he could not get it off! Fainting with exhaustion, Dushasana collapsed. Duryodhana ranted and raved at this failure; eventually storming out of the chambers. Although Krishna saved Draupadi from getting disgraced, he could not change the destiny of the Pandavas. At the end of it all, the Pandavas along with Draupadi were exiled to the forests for thirteen years.

Krishna is an Envoy

The relations between the Kauravas and the Pandavas turned uglier when the Pandavas successfully completed their period of exile and came back after thirteen years to reclaim all that they had lost. But Duryodhana refused to give them their kingdom back. Instead, he challenged them to war. This resulted in an exchange of envoys begging each side to maintain peace. Duryodhana blatantly refused all offers of a peaceful settlement. Finally, Krishna himself went to intervene and see if he could straighten out things between the Pandavas and the Kauravas.

That is how he arrived at the Kuru court and was granted an audience with the august Kuru leaders and Duryodhana. In the course of this mission, Krishna tried to come to a settlement for the Pandavas. However, Duryodhana opposed all his suggestions. Krishna did not give up. After Duryodhana had left the room, he began to put forth an effective argument to the elders on Duryodhana's misconduct. "It is one Duryodhana who stands between the Kuru race and disaster," Krishna passionately warned.

Hearing this, Duryodhana rushed back, shouting, "Seize Krishna, for he speaks ill of me and tries to turn my courtiers against me!" His brother Dushasana raced to seize Krishna. At that moment, Krishna worked a miracle again and suddenly he showed himself everywhere, in all things, even in the hearts of the people. Krishna actually split his image into many figures. Every corner seemed to be filled by a Krishna! Duryodhana and Dushashana desperately tried to catch the real Krishna whom they could not find! The courtiers present there had risen to their feet in protest at Duryodhana's insolence, since it was unheard of to treat an envoy this way! This is when Krishna allowed them to have a glimpse of his divine form, if only for a few seconds. They fell back in awe when they saw Krishna thus. Having made his point, Krishna disappeared in a puff of air and Duryodhana gnashed his teeth and glared at every one. In his unreasonable mind he still did not believe that Krishna had shown his divinity. "It is all a trick to let me down," muttered Duryodhana.

Krishna's Philosophy

No one could stop the Great War or the *Mahabharata* from happening. This war was fought at the famous battlefields of *Kurukshetra*. On one side, stood the Pandavas and their allies; and on the other side, the Kauravas with their allies. The five Pandavas and their allies were matched against the might of the huge Kaurava armies.

Krishna was Arjun's charioteer. Sitting on his chariot, Arjun gazed at the other side.

He could see his great uncle Bhishma, his teachers, Drona and Kripa, he saw all hundred of his Kaurava cousins. Suddenly, his heart flooded with remorse. He could not fight his own flesh and blood.

"I cannot fight. I cannot even think of killing my own kith and kin," Arjun sobbed with hands covering his face.

Krishna turned and flashed a worried look. This was not good. The war had not yet begun and Arjun already had cold feet. Krishna took charge of the situation and he started to make Arjun understand the reality of things. "Do your duty without any fear, without any desire or expectations. Arjun remember, it is not who you fight that is important but what you fight for!"

Krishna continued his discourse. The philosophy Krishna imparted kindled Arjun's mind. He listened raptly. Krishna's discourse to Arjun is called the *Bhagvad Gita*, which is Krishna's philosophy on duty and responsibility towards a better existence through the cycles of birth and rebirth. With a blinding light, Krishna revealed his true self to Arjun. He showed a limitless form, which to Arjun seemed infinite.

"I am so small compared to the pattern of existence," Arjun whispered in awe.

Krishna filled Arjun with a confidence he had never felt. Arjun was geared to face the challenge with guts and grit attributed to the true *Kshatriya*, fighting a just cause.

Arjun inclined his head and climbed on to his chariot. He was ready for the war. Arjun was always very close to Krishna. In fact, Krishna had married his sister Subhadra to Arjun. Subhadra and Arjun had a son named Abhimanyu.

The End of Duryodhana

The Pandavas, after many days of mayhem and destruction, won the war. First their great uncle Bhishma fell, then their teacher, Drona. These two were aligned to the Kauravas. Then, one by one, the Kaurava allies and all hundred Kaurava brothers, except Duryodhana, were vanquished. Finally, Duryodhana was fleeing for his life, hotly pursued by the avenging Pandavas.

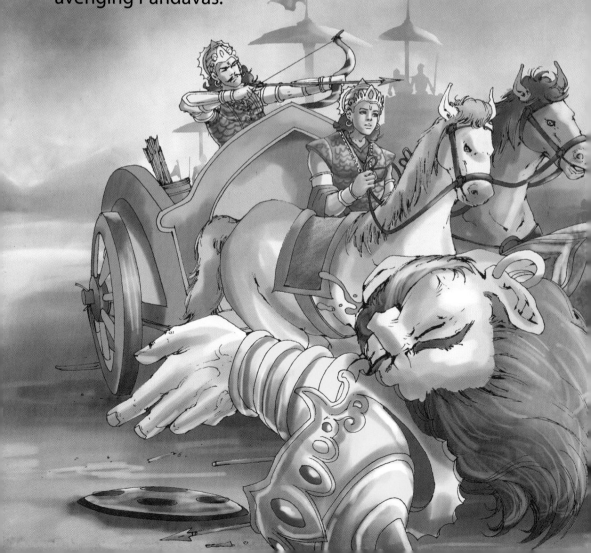

Duryodhana could not run for long. He met his nemesis at the hands of Bhima. Even as Duryodhana lay dying, he had no repentance. The Pandavas won this war with Krishna's help. He had become their close ally as he guided them with expert strategies. However, the war caused so much of devastation that when Pandavas returned to claim their inheritance at Hastinapur, they were broken and sad men. This victory meant little to them. They had lost much more.

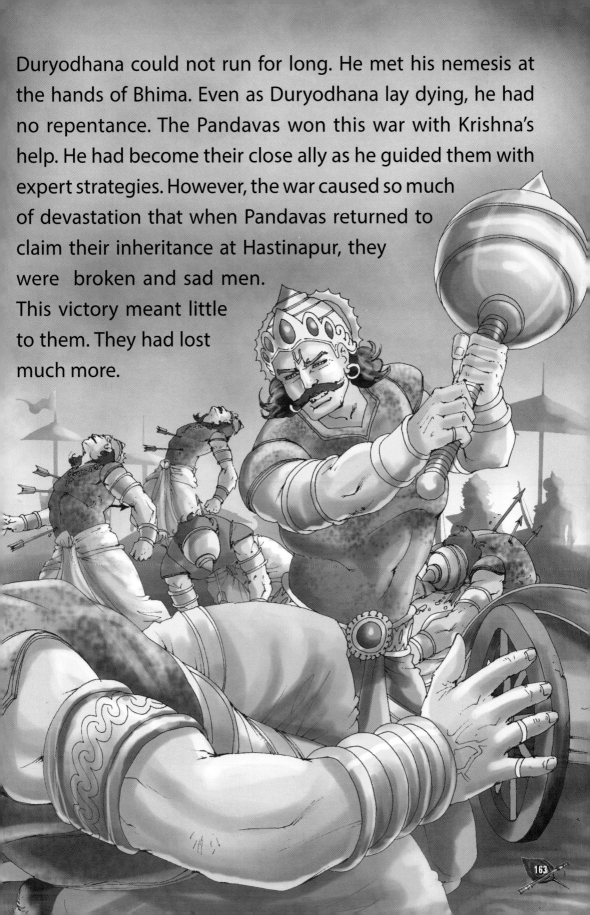

Ashwathama's Revenge

Ashwathama, Guru Drona's son, wanted to avenge his father's death. He sneaked into the Pandava camp and slit the throat of all present, including Draupadi's sons. He could not slay the Pandavas or Draupadi, because they were not in the camp at that time. Once this heinous crime was discovered, the Pandavas chased Ashwathama through the moorlands he took refuge in. Powered by some strong magical knowledge, Ashwathama picked up a blade and rubbed a spell into it.

With this as a weapon, he threw it at the Pandavas. They successfully evaded it; Ashwathama turned his blade of grass into a curse and shouted that no heirs of the Pandavas would survive. He flung the blade with this curse. It ricocheted from the Pandavas, took the shape of a dagger and aimed at Princess Uttara's womb, which was carrying Abhimanyu's unborn child. Krishna anticipating this, extended his hand and deflected the blade and stalled the disaster. Uttara eventually gave birth to a son who was named Parikshit. Parikshit eventually inherited the throne of Hastinapur after the Pandavas.

Krishna Leaves his Body

Finally, Krishna returned to Dwarka. His days became occupied as the challenges of running a kingdom kept him busy. One day, Krishna, decided to rest awhile in the forest.

He found a cool and isolated spot. Not faraway, a hunter was hunting for deer. The hunter saw Krishna's left heel and mistook it for the head of a deer. 'Aha, a deer,' thought the hunter and with an expert twang, he shot an arrow which hit its mark. The fatal arrow hit the centre of Krishna's heel where his life was centered. The hunter on finding out his mistake, rushed to Krishna. He sobbed, asking for forgiveness.

With life ebbing from him, Krishna hushed him and whispered forgiving words, "It is time for me to leave. Do not blame yourself." Then, in a final sigh, Krishna's soul left his body to return to heaven. Even as his soul transported itself, the forest was filled with the music of his flute and the heady fragrance of flowers.